SPACS INVESTING 101

*The Original Beginner's Guide
to all the Pros and Cons of*
Special Purpose Acquisition Companies.

Make the right investment today!

**OSCAR WILLIAMS
ROBERT HAMILTON**

© Copyright 2021 by Oscar Williams & Robert Hamilton - All rights reserved.

The following Book is reproduced below with the goal of providing information that is as accurate and reliable as possible. Regardless, purchasing this Book can be seen as consent to the fact that both the publisher and the author of this book are in no way experts on the topics discussed within and that any recommendations or suggestions that are made herein are for entertainment purposes only. Professionals should be consulted as needed prior to undertaking any of the action endorsed herein.

This declaration is deemed fair and valid by both the American Bar Association and the Committee of Publishers Association and is legally binding throughout the United States.

Furthermore, the transmission, duplication, or reproduction of any of the following work including specific information will be considered an illegal act irrespective of if it is done electronically or in print. This extends to creating a secondary or tertiary copy of the work or a recorded copy and is only allowed with the express written consent from the Publisher. All additional right reserved.

The information in the following pages is broadly considered a truthful and accurate account of facts and as such, any inattention, use, or misuse of the information in question by the reader will render any resulting actions solely under their purview. There are no scenarios in which the publisher or the original author of this work can be in any fashion deemed liable for any hardship or damages that may befall them after undertaking information described herein.

Additionally, the information in the following pages is intended only for informational purposes and should thus be thought of as universal. As befitting its nature, it is presented without assurance regarding its prolonged validity or interim quality. Trademarks that are mentioned are done without written consent and can in no way be considered an endorsement from the trademark holder.

Table of Contents

INTRODUCTION 5

SPECIAL PURPOSE ACQUISITION COMPANIES (SPACS): WHAT EXACTLY ARE THEY? 9

WHAT ARE THE MOST SIGNIFICANT SPACS' BENEFITS? 13

THE HISTORY OF SPACS 16

SPACS: WHY DO THEY EXIST? 22

SPACS: HOW DO THEY WORK? 26

SPACS: WHAT ARE THE PROS? 36

SPACS: WHAT ARE THE CONS? 38

SPACS VS. IPOS 46

SPAC DEAL: WHAT KIND OF COMPANY MAKES THE BEST CANDIDATE? 53

SPACS INVESTING: THE DIFFERENT STAGES OF THE DEAL 55

SPACS INVESTING: THE MOST IMPORTANT TIPS FOR BEGINNERS 61

WHERE INVESTORS CAN BUY SPACS 68

SPAC TRENDS IN 2021 71

CONCLUSIONS 75

INTRODUCTION

Nowadays, it is hard to keep up with all the trends and fads of our overheated investment world. Even so, the rise of special purpose acquisition companies, or SPACs, hasn't gone unnoticed by almost anyone.

Why? Well, numbers speak for themselves.

The SPACs' boom started in 2020 when they accounted for almost 42% of the overall IPO market value and more than 50% of all IPOs. Pretty impressive, especially considering that back in 2017, when CII first started tracking SPACs, they represented just 2% of the total market and 7% of IPOs value. According to the information of SPAC Insider, in the year 2020, 247 newly formed SPACs raised a total of $83 billion in capital through initial public offerings. And in 2019 and 2020 alone, more Special Purpose Acquisition Companies were created than in the prior 18 years altogether.

Not only the number of these companies is increasing, but also SPACs are raising more funds through IPOs to allow them to purchase bigger private companies. In 2020, the average SPAC IPO was more than $335 million compared to "only" $230 million in the previous exercise.

Also, the global value of the total SPACs listed in the U.S. surged as the number of deals rose an impressive 1,000% from 2016 to 2020.
The overall value of SPAC deals completed between 2019 and 2020 skyrocketed 400%, according to Dealogic's information. And so far, in 2021, the amount of completed deals already totals more than 50% of those carried out in the previous fiscal year.
Now bankers say this blockbuster trend is making its way across the Atlantic. Recently, the former chief of

UniCredit, one of the most important Italian banks, teamed up with the founder of Louis Vuitton handbag maker LVMH to launch a SPAC aimed at buying a European financial company. And Klaus Hommels, one of Spotify's first investors, launched his own tech-focused SPAC in Frankfurt, Germany's financial core.

Indeed, it looks like SPAC's booming is expanding to the rest of the world.

Nowadays, there are an impressive number of European and Asia-Pacific companies that would want to be listed but rather do it in their own regions. So for these companies, it is important that there might also be a local SPAC offering in the upcoming future.

And there is no reason to think that the actual SPACs' parameters shouldn't be widely employed in places like Paris, Stockholm, Frankfurt, Amsterdam, London, and all the other key listings locations in the Old Continent. Also, there is undoubtedly a deep enough pool of capital for that. And this is because there is huge demand from both European and global investors.

Because of these impressive numbers and movements, it is crucial for investors to properly understand how special purpose acquisition companies work and their main characteristics (for both the good and the bad). Some of them, for example, are interesting to operating companies and SPAC sponsors but not necessarily to investors. Others may just turn out to be an investor's next big, profitable deal.

The purpose of this book is to guide you through the most significant information about SPACs, their benefits and risks, and everything you should take into account before considering your next investment. Because, as you will see, when you decide to invest in special purpose acquisition companies, you don't really know what you are going to get.

But what we do know for sure is that there are plenty of opportunities developing in the SPAC sector right now. Might this mean an oversupply of SPAC deals? Are most of them going to fail? Probably. But investors that do the hard work of finding the best ones can be rewarded exceptionally well...

So, shall we begin?

Special Purpose Acquisition Companies (SPACs): What Exactly Are They?

Special Purpose Acquisition Companies or SPACs are publicly listed non-operating companies whose goal is to recognize and purchase a private company, allowing their acquisition target to have publicly listed stock.
A significant minority of SPACs are formed without a specific industry focus, keeping their options open about how to invest the IPO funds: they represent about 20% of the total number of SPACs launched since January 1st, 2020.
But the great majority of SPACs are already formed with a specific target industry in mind. This is why the SPAC's management team and sponsors generally have (actually... should have!) experience in that particular area.

SPACs are also called "blank check" companies. In other words, a SPAC is a vehicle that is listed on a particular exchange — it could be here, in the United States, but as we said, also in Europe. And that vehicle's objective is essentially, in a fixed amount of time, to consummate an acquisition of a private company causing this one to become a listed company in its own right effectively.

When a SPAC or other publicly traded company purchases a private one, this is called a reverse merger, opposite to a traditional merger that takes place when a private company takes a public company private.

And what about SPACs' value? When investors buy traditional shares, they are taking a stake in a company that offers services or goods to consumers or businesses. So, profits, revenues, dividends, etc., can measure the quality of that company.
But the potential benefit of a SPAC cannot be calculated like that because, as we said, they basically are "cash shell"

businesses that have no commercial operations at all, even though they have been listed on the stock market.
This means that when you invest in SPACs, you trust the sponsors to find a good target to merge with at some point.

It is overall believed that, through a SPAC transaction, a private company can become a publicly traded one with more certainty in terms of pricing and control over the terms of the transaction compared to IPOs.
These kinds of transactions, in which a SPAC typically acquires or merges with a private company, take place after several months or even more than a year after the SPAC has completed its own IPO. However, unlike an operating company that goes public through a traditional IPO, a SPAC has no underlying operating business and no assets other than cash and limited investments, including proceeds from the IPO.

Normally, in fact, a company starts and grows a business. Over time, that company may expand to the point where it determines that it has the resources and structures necessary for the IPO process, as well as subsequent SEC reporting requirements, and chooses to seek to raise capital in the public markets, thereby becoming a public company.
Public companies can list their securities on an exchange.
But as we just said, if you invest in a SPAC at the initial public offering stage, you decide to put your faith in the management team that has formed the SPAC, also called the sponsor(s), as the SPAC tries to acquire or merge with an operating company. That acquisition or combination is called an "initial business combination." Even though a SPAC may indicate in its IPO prospectus a specific sector or business that it plans to pursue when seeking to combine with an operating company, it is not legally required to pursue a target in that

particular field (we will talk more about this in the following pages).

When the SPAC has identified an initial business combination opportunity, its management negotiates with the operating company. If approved by SPAC's shareholders (whenever a shareholder vote is required), the business combination occurs.
This transaction, as indicated, is usually structured as a reverse merger in which the operating company merges with a SPAC or a subsidiary of a SPAC. Although there are several ways to structure the initial business combination, the combined company after the transaction is a publicly-traded one and continues the business of the target operating company.

What Are The Most Significant SPACs' Benefits?

This question might have more than one answer, mostly because it depends on whom you are asking. The appeal of a SPAC is actually different for each market participant.

SPAC sponsors are those who bring the Special Purpose Acquisition Companies to market and choose which company to target, easily gaining access to capital and the flexibility to deploy it as they see fit. The majority of SPAC sponsors are investment professionals, financial market or esteemed business executives with industry expertise. To all of them, SPACs are a much easier way of raising and investing capital than through a venture capital fund or formal private equity. SPACs also present a potentially lucrative exit since SPAC sponsors receive a share of equity in any company they merge with.

SPAC investors, on the other hand, are those who buy up shares in the listed SPAC before a merger target is identified, and they benefit from the significant potential upside of a finalized transaction, and risk-free conditions before any merger is completed.
That is because all IPO funds are placed in an interest-bearing trust account: that money can only be used to complete acquisitions. Therefore, if a deal never goes through, investors can recoup the investment they made with just a relatively small interest return.

And then, merging with a SPAC is a quite simple way to list on a public stock exchange for private companies. At least, easier than with an initial public offering. The traditional IPO way is a long and difficult process that involves filing a lot of paperwork with the SEC and wooing investors. Compared to all this, merging with a SPAC is pretty simple. Another benefit? A company's initial IPO price can swing back and forth in the previous hours to the listing as bankers calculate the demand of the investors. With SPACs, on the other hand, you agree upon in advance the company's valuation, offering more stability to existing shareholders and founders.

Finally, investors in a private company – generally private equity funds and venture capital – also benefit. Why? Because SPAC deals typically price higher than traditional IPOs and private transactions.

The History of SPACs

The very first SPAC goes all the way back to 1993, but it was only in 1994 when special purpose acquisition companies really took off: according to SPAC Research, with a record 248 issues raising almost $84 billion, up from 59 in the previous exercise.

The action continued into 2020, with an impressive $117 billion of SPAC mergers and $35.3 billion of IPOs in February that marked a new record.
The COVID-19 pandemic gave a great boost to SPACS because lockdown restrictions made it almost impossible to pursue a traditional IPO, which implies several processes when a company goes public. These include, for example, choosing an investment bank to advise on the offering, due filings and diligence, roadshows and pricing, and so on.

According to the vice director at Swissquote Bank Dubai, Chaddy Kirbaj, SPACs are a relatively simple and rapid way to raise funds for a private company, as a SPAC merger may take just 3 or 4 months (even if, as we will see later, it might be some more than what it looks like) opposite to the usual six months of a traditional IPO.

We could say that SPAC mergers are basically the direct-to-consumer version of IPOs. They don't have the same huge number of middlemen in the process, and so they are less expensive, quicker, and imply less legal oversight.
This allows private investors the opportunity to enter the imposing world of private equity, whose access was previously restricted to the big financial players such as investment banks and hedge funds.

But that access has a price since, as we will see in a few pages, the dice are loaded in favor of the SPAC's sponsors, who pay a nominal amount for the biggest slice of the shares.
Also, private companies that go public via a SPAC merger generally face way less scrutiny than those that go through a traditional IPO.

So basically, SPACs offers investors access to experienced management and capital, and their board is generally composed of high-profile personalities with hedge fund and private equity experience.

Exactly what happened in 2019, when Richard Branson's commercial spaceflight operation Virgin Galactic announced that it would go public. But that they wouldn't do it through a traditional IPO. Instead, they would be merging with a Special Purpose Acquisition Company backed by billionaire V.C. investor and former Facebook exec Chamath Palihapitiya.
This announcement started the so-called "SPAC revolution" and offered the SPAC market its long-overdue attention. Because despite their interesting benefits, for years, SPACs had been shunned on Wall Street as "taboo." It is like IPOs were the only way to go for legitimate companies with serious operations.
But the Virgin Galactic SPAC merge in July 2019 forever changed that status quo. The fact that such a strong, high-profile, well-funded company had chosen this way to go made it clear that SPACs were the real deal, and that taboo feeling about SPACs finally began to fade away, giving them, for the very first time, the legitimacy they deserved.

Then, only five months later, also DraftKings, the sports betting giant, chose to go public through a SPAC instead of an IPO.

And guess what? Both Virgin Galactic and DraftKings' mergers went incredibly well, allowing companies and their early shareholders to make tons of money.

Starting from there, it was like during 2020, every small company with a good idea decided to go public with a SPAC, appreciating all the benefits (overall, easier funding and better valuation) that come with the fact of being a public company.
Since the beginning of last year, 118 SPACs have closed on an acquisition, representing more than $120 billion of public value. Pretty impressive for a market that was closing about ten deals per year just twenty-four months before.

But then, as often happens, this SPAC boom turned into a SPAC bubble, and then in a SPAC crash.

The sector also came under incremented regulatory scrutiny, threatening to make many proposed mergers more arduous. This is why many investors decided to completely forget about the market, labeling SPAC stocks as "dead money."
Are they right? The truth is, it doesn't really look like it.

Because after the 2021 SPAC crash, there are tons of potentially life-changing opportunities out there... exactly like it happened in 2002, after the Dot-Com Crash, when several investment opportunities made dip-buyers millionaires over the following twenty years.
Also, the news that the U.S. Securities and Exchange Commission will prepare tighter regulations and that scared off some investors, could also turn out to be a positive thing since it will reduce risks and improve the quality of management teams.

In other words, in the search for the next Netflix, Amazon, or Google, it might be a very good idea to start looking at the SPAC "cemetery."

Because even though there are many questionable companies in this market (no, we won't deny that), we can also find some of the most pioneering in the world. Companies that might have the potential to change the way the world works and the way all of us live, just like Virgin Galactic and its ground-breaking space tourism.

This is a natural and obvious by-product of the SPAC structure, which allows brand new companies to sell their vision, project, and technology and receive funding to materialize, execute, and commercialize their ideas.

It's like V.C. investing. In this market, you see losers everywhere, but you can also find some real winners. And if you choose the right V.C. investment, you will end up creating real wealth.
So basically, the same applies to the SPAC market. Nowadays, all SPAC stocks, no matter their quality, are getting crushed. This unselective selling has created an amazing buying opportunity in innovative companies that are now trading at incredible discounts. So SPACs are far from dead. Including Rishi Sunak, UK Chancellor is currently reviewing how to introduce them into the City of London in order to boost start-ups of the tech field.

But to find the best SPAC stocks to buy, it is crucial to be very selective and only invest in the top-quality SPACs in the market. The most challenging thing for investors is that they have absolutely no idea what the company is being created for, what they will end up financing, and where their money will go. So buying SPACs'shares is somehow like a leap of faith. And this secrecy is aimed to avoid informing rival bidders.

Luckily, investors are not totally blind, though, since SPACs should still make public a statement of intent, indicating the region or industry of their target, and name the SPAC sponsors and founding investors. Anyhow, considering the secrecy surrounding these operations, it's extremely important to carry out a careful diligence, examining previous performance and backgrounds of the different SPAC sponsors and the industries they are targeting in order to measure their potential. It is crucial to carefully consider factors such as SPAC size, target industry, and an all-star management team. But watch out... all-star doesn't mean "celebrity"!

Actually investors should stay as far apart as possible from SPACs that recruit VIPs as sponsors. A few examples? Shaquille O'Neal, Jay-Z, Serena Williams, and Larry Kudlow are all out there promoting launches.

Well, in the next chapters of this guide, we will talk in more detail about all this in order to understand exactly how SPACs work, their benefits and risks, and what should be taken into account to make an informed decision and carry out a great investment.

SPACs: Why Do They Exist?

Let's start from the basics.

As we briefly mentioned before, private companies are willing to be acquired by SPACs because it is overall less problematic and more flexible than going public through an IPO.

The financial markets' openness to new public offerings, changes depending on investors' risk appetite and economic conditions. SPACs are already public, so a reverse merger permits a private company to go public when the IPO window is shut.

SPAC acquisitions are also appealing to private companies because, in a reverse merger, their principal shareholders and founders may sell a higher percentage of their ownership than they could with an IPO.

Also, private company founders have the opportunity to avoid the lock-up periods for selling newly public shares that are mandatory for IPOs.

And then, one of the main reasons such an impressive number of SPACs was able to go public in the last few months is basically that it has been very easy for them to raise funds. And this is because, as we will see later in greater detail, when investors put their money in a SPAC and eventually this doesn't close a deal, they will recover a certain minimum amount of money, which normally is $10. SPACs' sponsors must return investors those funds, minus some expenses, if they can't close a deal in the indicated time (generally, 24 months).

Consequently, several large investors and hedge funds have subscribed to almost every possible SPAC because they didn't present any real risk. They had the possibility to acquire units at $10, knowing that they could redeem them at close to $10 at some point if no deal were closed in the following months.

Furthermore, the best SPACs have the capability of substantial upside. And to prove that, we just have to think about what happened with QuantumScape, which jumped from $10 to more than $130 at its peak, and DraftKings, which is up 700% since its SPAC inception.

With the potential for SPACs to double or more and risks limited to $10, there is no doubt we find ourselves in the presence of an asymmetrical risk pattern. Downsides do exist, of course, but if you are able to spot the next SPAC with a potential hot deal (maybe the most complicated thing to do), there is also a potentially very big upside.

Due to the flood of pre-trade SPACs coming to market, more and more of them are currently trading at a little premium over the $10 redemption price.

A few months ago, on the other hand, many of the pre-transaction SPACs were trading higher due to the great optimism of the investors that considered that a deal would be struck. That optimism has faded away, but that makes for better entry points for those investors determined to look for the best SPACs out there.

In general, the main risk for SPAC holders is opportunity cost. It can take months or even years for a SPAC to find a deal if it finds one at all. The holding costs for these

SPACs may not be very high in today's low-interest-rate environment, but the funds will have dead money on their books if there is no deal.

The good thing? With the price of several new SPACs pretty close to their $10 redemption levels because of apprehension over a possible oversupply of pre-IPO SPACs, we have some potential opportunities for small investors who are normally left out of the IPO process.

This means that today it is possible to play like sophisticated hedge funds by holding a number of SPACs with overall small downside risk and the possibility of large upside potential if the right names are chosen.
With like five well-selected SPACs, there is a good chance that at least one ends up closing a deal, and others might make moves on a possible agreement.

To recap, the thing is buying a basket of SPACs that trade near their $10 redemption price and hope that some of them might hit it big and make up for the relatively small losses that occur when other SPACs sell off or close at the redemption price. One or two winners will probably more than makeup for the losses of these small losers.
The big challenge is to find those few winners...

SPACs: How Do They Work?

To properly understand SPACs' functioning, let's analyze below the typical structure of a Special Purpose Acquisition Company:

Founders' Shares and Units (Sponsors vs Investors)

SPAC sponsors typically acquire capital in the SPAC on more favorable terms than IPO investors or subsequent investors in the open market. This is why investors should know that even though IPO investors have contributed the majority of the SPAC's capital, sponsors and potentially other initial investors will benefit more than them from the SPAC's execution of an initial business combination. And that they might want to complete a transaction under conditions that may be less favorable to investors.
Furthermore, SPACs could need extra financings to fund the initial business combination, and those kinds of movements typically involve sponsors. Consequently, the sponsors' interests may differ even further from investors'.
For all these reasons it is extremely important to look for more information about a sponsor's interests in a SPAC in the "Principal Shareholders" and "Certain Relationships and Related Party Transactions" sections of the IPO prospectus of a SPAC.
It is also possible to get more information about an initial business combination and the sponsor's interests in it in the proxy statement, information statement, or tender offer statement. This is crucial to understand if SPAC investors' incentives are overall aligned with SPAC sponsors' incentives.

So, before the IPO, SPAC's sponsors purchase initial equity, often referred to as "Founder Shares" or "Promoter

Shares," for a nominal value and acquire additional warrants to help fund start-up costs and fees.

They are in charge of the management of the SPAC through the de-SPAC merger. This includes searching for an interesting private operating company, managing working capital, finding more funders, and negotiating the deal's price.

This arrangement is a totally different thing from the SPAC shares or units that investors purchase. In fact, sponsors make a nominal contribution, known as a "promote," in exchange for this stake, which is at risk of loss just in case the SPAC finally fails in acquiring a target company and has to liquidate. The promote raises a meager amount of capital for an important stake— generally $25,000 for 20% of the SPAC's equity. While sponsors may inject more capital, the key imbalance for SPAC investors to understand is that they assume most of the cost of searching for and acquiring a target company and most of the risk of losing the invested capital. These risks and rewards are the same no matter the quality of the target company, the valuation the SPAC sponsor negotiates for it or the target's success as a public company.

In connection with the SPAC's IPO and during a posterior period of time, investors may buy units composed of one share of common stock and a warrant to purchase stock in the upcoming future. Normally, the unit price starts at $10.

SPAC IPO investors count on a guaranteed return of interest if they decide to redeem their shares and also any upside from free warrants. The units trade for 52 days before "splitting" into separate, independently traded securities. Thirty days after the de-SPAC merger, warrants become exercisable for between one-quarter and one share, typically at an exercise price of $11.50/share. Some units also include rights to additional fractional shares at no cost.

Sponsors generally consider the promote compensation for the SPAC's managing more than just an investment. Yet, talking about risks, there is still a huge difference between SPAC sponsors and investors and some dynamics typical of this market also exacerbate this divergence.

Investors generally have a somehow more substantial interest in having the SPAC making a favorable acquisition. Sponsors on the other hand, have a stronger interest in just finalizing a purchase.

This misalignment of risk is the same for every SPAC, including those led by important and well-regarded sponsors with significant experience. To make an example, Michael Klein, former Citigroup banker, and his team received a $275 million promote for $25,000 before merging the Churchill Capital Corp with MultiPlan Corporation, a health care service company. It was a record SPAC merger, and since then, the NYSE-listed stock has taken a hit since revelations following the de-SPAC. Still, the promote arrangement nearly assures upside for the sponsor.

As indicated before, a SPAC generally commits in its prospectus to closing a business combination within two years. If the deal is not completed in that period of time, the capital raised from the IPO is given back to investors and the SPAC is dissolved. And this is a terrible outcome for a sponsor, considering the depleted trust account funds the acquisition and the operating expenses of the SPAC. And these are often partially financed by the purchase of warrants of the sponsor.

So, considering the pretty inflexible timeframe to acquire an operating company, sponsors really do have a strong incentive to close a deal, even if the company's prospects are somehow questionable.

This risk especially rises when there is rapid growth in the number of SPACs that outstrip the supply of high-quality private operating companies willing to go public. While this world of supply and demand may have some positive benefits for public investors (like, for example, sponsors reducing their promote or establishing some innovative terms to catch the attention of operating firms), deteriorating deal access stemming from greater competition may spur a sponsor to strike merger agreements with targets they could pass up in a less-over crowded market.

So, generally speaking, these differing interests may damage investors as managers evaluate potential acquisition targets before the SPAC's liquidation date.

Warrants

Sponsor and public warrants (i.e., unit warrants) generally have the same terms and cannot be exercised until after the business combination transaction with an operating company is completed. Sponsor warrants are generally exercisable on a net basis (public warrants generally are not) and might be recoverable for cash or shares on a formula basis. Public and sponsor warrants (or both of them) could be subject to a formula redemption for cash or stock to clear a public company's cap table.

This means that a SPAC may redeem warrants in accordance with its terms. And the terms of warrants can vary widely among SPACs.

Knowing when warrants can be redeemed and whether they will be redeemed can mark the difference between a worthwhile investment and a bad one. In case of not receiving the redemption notice and not exercising it within the prescribed period, warrants may become virtually worthless. But since not in every case timely warrants notice of redemption are communicated directly, it is important to consult a financial professional to always be aware of how such notices can be obtained. On the SEC's EDGAR database, it is possible to stay informed about redemptions of warrants.

Trust Account

An important capital portion (85% or even more) raised through the IPO process is placed in an interest-bearing trust account during the SPAC search/combination period. SPACs normally have to negotiate into all contracts a waiver of any claims against the trust to prevent trust funds from being used for any purpose before the completion of an acquisition. The sponsor has a limited ability to use the interest generated by the trust to help fund working capital.

Target Size

The value of the possible target business combination generally should at least represent a minimum of 80% of the trust's assets. Accordingly, most target values exceed available cash (on average, three to four times), and the form of consideration for the transaction is both cash and shares of the SPAC.

Search Period

SPACs typically have 18 to 24 months after the IPO to identify a target company and submit it to the shareholders' vote. SPACs usually have to hold a shareholder vote on a proposed resolution prior to the deadline or their governing documents will require an automatic dissolution of the SPAC and the trust account, unless the SPAC's shareholders approve an extension of that deadline. Note that this requires some lead time for a Form S-4 or general proxy solicitation to be prepared and declared effective, so the actual time to enter into an agreement is a few months less. As previously indicated, sponsors lose their investment if a target is not found within this period.

Shareholder Redemption

You should know by now that a fundamental SPACs' feature is that shareholders are entitled to redeem their shares when voting on any business combination or amendments to the governing documents (like, for example, to extend the search period).
Shareholders are normally required to approve the business combination at the shareholders' meeting, and those who choose to redeem their shares receive money from the trust account equal to the initial public offering price plus accrued interest but retain their warrants. Some SPACs include restrictions on individual shareholders redeeming large blocks of shares (e.g., 15% of outstanding shares).
On the other hand, at the moment of the vote, shareholders who have a favorable opinion of the potential initial business combination and its valuation may decide to remain on board and be shareholders of the combined company. When this happens, the combination called "De-SPAC transaction" starts, and the target business combines into the publicly traded company.
When special purpose acquisition companies seek approval from the shareholders about this initial business combination, they provide them with a proxy statement prior to their vote. In cases where a SPAC does not seek public shareholder approval because some stockholders, such as the sponsor and

the affiliates, have sufficient votes to approve the transaction, it will provide the shareholders with an information statement before the consummation of the initial business combination.

The information or proxy statement should include important information about the business of the company the SPAC seeks to acquire, such as the company's financial statements, the interests of the parties to the transaction, including SPAC's sponsors, and the terms of the of the initial business combination transaction.

In case a SPAC is not required to provide shareholders with an information statement or a proxy (like in the case of a SPAC not required to count on shareholder approval for the transaction), investors will receive a tender offer statement containing information about the transaction target company and their redemption rights.

Some supporters of the SPAC route to IPO point to de-SPAC merger shareholder redemption rights as an attractive safeguard for investors. These can limit downside exposure by reviewing the information in the de-SPAC merger proxy and redeeming their shares for their original offering price plus accrued interest if they do not see a captivating transaction.

This is an important protection for the investors. But how reliable really is the information they review?

The redemption decision is difficult in part due to the uncertainty surrounding the reliability of projections about the future earnings and revenue prospects of the combined company. Investors should be aware that the legal community is engaged in an active conversation about the consequences for target companies and SPAC sponsors and target companies of too few or too selective forward-looking projections.

The Securities and Exchange Commission (SEC) recently called into question what was a widespread assumption that

the liability risk in de-SPAC proxy statements was less than that of traditional IPOs.
It is widely accepted that the SPAC IPO itself carries the same strict liability under Section 11 of the Securities Act for omissions and misstatements that apply to a normal IPO. But the prevailing view has been that SPAC disclosures about the operating company carry less liability because they are covered by the "safe harbor" for forward-looking statements in the Private Securities Litigation Reform Act (PSLRA) of 1995.1.

Actually, someone seems to consider this "safe harbor" not safe at all. In recent declarations, John Coates, acting director of the SEC's Division of Corporation Finance, indicated that any statement about reduced liability exposure for participants in SPACs was overstated at best and potentially misleading at worst. According to him, in some ways, the liability risks to participants are greater, not less, than in conventional IPOs, especially due to the potential conflicts of interest in the SPAC structure.
Coates stated that the Private Securities Litigation Reform Act does not define the term "initial public offering," and the legislative history includes statements that the safe harbor was intended for 'seasoned issuers' with an established track record. The result, in his opinion, is that the PSLRA excludes from its safe harbor initial public offerings, and that phrase can therefore include de-SPAC transactions.

In general, you should remember that the most common SPAC IPO structure is made of a Class A common stock share united with a warrant. This provides the holder with the right to buy more stock at a later date and at a fixed price.
Investors who participate in this are generally happy to have the possibility to exercise the warrants in order to get more

common stock shares when the acquisition target is determined, and the transaction closes.

Normally, the IPO price for a SPAC stock is $10/share. The exercise price for the warrants is normally set at about 15% (or higher) than the initial public offering price.

A few weeks later, the warrant can trade separately from the SPAC stock, and at least 85% of the SPAC IPO proceeds have to be put in an escrow account for another acquisition. The remaining amount is held in reserve to cover IPO underwriting expenses and SPAC's operating fees, like due diligence, accounting, and legal expenses.

Typically, funds in the escrow account will be invested in government bonds.

SPACs: What Are The Pros?

Overall, in the previous pages of this book, we have largely talked about the most advantageous and innovative SPACs' features. So below, we will briefly highlight the main positive characteristics of a SPAC, and then we will focus a little more extensively on its downsides. We are witnessing the rise of an exciting trend, but in order to make smart decisions, it is crucial to have the full picture of SPAC investing, with all the good and all the bad that comes with it.

So, the first important characteristic of a SPAC is its flexibility. Everything can be negotiated, and sponsorships shares can be adjusted from 20% to 0% too.
The negotiations on warrants and shares are open, particularly when the termination date is approaching. Another positive point is access to primary capital.
Timing is also very important. As briefly mentioned before, a traditional IPO takes about six months to start trading, while a SPAC only takes an average of three months.

SPACs: What Are The Cons?

Possible Low Transparency

There is a good reason vetting of a public company is slow. And this is why one of the most significant SPAC's benefits can also make it a risky operation. The typical timeframe for a de-SPAC is 10 weeks. In comparison, a traditional IPO usually takes 19 weeks, even though the preparation for IPOs often widens this gap: a quick-moving public offering might imply a simplified paperwork process but low transparency too. Also, investors should be aware that a faster timeline may attract a group of operating companies that are disproportionately focused on capitalizing on a hot market, hot sector, or "fads."

Too Much Decision-Making Power In The Sponsors' Hands

It is the valuation method of the SPAC process that operating companies find attractive but that, once again, may also implies significant risks.
Companies can negotiate with a single counterparty, the SPAC sponsor, representing a large block of capital, rather than risk the volatility that comes with having underwriters and a book processing the shares and voting in favor of the merger to ensure that their warrants are not worthless.
In addition, depending on the SPAC ownership profile, SPAC mergers can be approved without the majority support of the SPAC's public shareholders because of the voting power exercised by the sponsors, including supervoting rights for certain classes. Therefore, in some cases, no application is required because the sponsor and its affiliates can meet the threshold for approval without the support of SPAC's public shareholders.

SPAC merger proxies are sometimes distributed less than 14 days in advance of the meeting date, reducing the opportunity to dissect the deal. According to ISS data, since 2010, not a single proposal to approve a SPAC-related transaction has failed to pass.

Investors accustomed to voting on an M&A deal typically expect company boards to get at least a fair opinion, if not more. A SPAC board has good reason to obtain an outside opinion on the fairness of the deal for an illiquid company, especially considering that directors are typically paid through a transfer of shares of stock from the sponsors. However, there are examples of SPAC boards omitting a third-party valuation or fairness opinion, just citing the sponsor's experience and qualifications. As the acquisition deadline approaches, SPAC sponsors that feel under pressure to close a deal may look outside the original scope to avoid liquidation. For example, Leisure Acquisition Corporation originally indicated that it would seek a leisure company, but in the end, it acquired a clinical-stage biotechnology company. Stable Road Acquisition Corporation at first disclosed it was looking for a cannabis company but ultimately pursued a space exploration company. Investors contemplating redeeming their shares in these pivot situations will have to decide if to go for the new opportunity and close a deal within 24 months after an unsuccessful pursuit of targets. Anyhow, depending on the circumstances, tolerance of a pivot can also end up being useful for them. To make an example, after the 2008 financial crisis, some non-real estate SPACs were converted to REITs. As the originally expected opportunities had evaporated, the change made sense while significant real estate assets were available at low prices.

High Dilution

The SPAC process often results in substantial dilution, the extent of which SPAC investors are not aware of until after the business combination. The promote is only one of the costs that dilute the money raised in the SPAC process.
Warrants to purchase shares in the future, rights to purchase additional shares at no cost, and underwriting fees become more expensive for SPAC shareholders who remain during the merger as the number of redemptions increases. A fundamental problem for SPAC investors is that the actual degree of dilution is unknown until after they have decided whether to redeem their shares or not.
SPAC merger "minimum-maximum" statements describing the impact of dilution in zero and 100% payback scenarios are of limited utility, as SPAC paybacks typically fall somewhere between those extremes.
Some researchers estimate that, as a result of all dilution deals, for the median SPAC, the $10 raised per share is reduced to $6.67 at the time of the SPAC merger, and that, in effect, SPAC investors are simply subsidizing the operating company.
Recently, some SPACs have contained some of the dilution associated with this route to IPO. For example, a legacy unit model that included a buy order for a full share has diminished over time to a fraction of a share, and some SPACs now mandate the SPAC option to redeem outstanding warrants.

Substantial Underwriting Costs

Underwriting costs might also be higher than you might think. For SPAC IPOs, these fees are based on a percentage of the proceeds raised, just as in traditional IPOs. However, it is important to note that, due to the redemption phase of a SPAC, the cash raised may be different from the cash received. The nominal fee percentage is usually lower in SPACs than the classic 7% fee in traditional IPOs. It is unusual for SPAC underwriting commissions to be adjusted for redemptions at the time of the de-SPAC. Without adjustment, that "appealing" 5% underwriting fee with a 50% redemption rate is equivalent to the merged company paying 10%.

Inexperienced Sponsors And Advisors

As we said, SPAC sponsors and affiliates can provide valuable leadership, visibility, both, or neither. Actually, some SPAC managers have a deep history of leadership in the sector on which the SPAC intends to focus its search. And other sponsors have financial expertise and connections to additional capital that may prove crucial during the SPAC process; we would be talking, for example, about private investors, private equity funds, and hedge funds. Not surprisingly, SPACs, where management has a history of financial or industry insight, have been more successful than other SPACs.

But the ease of starting up a SPAC and the low initial capital required have attracted sponsors and advisors from diverse backgrounds, sometimes with little experience in finance or the industry in question. Inexperienced sponsors and advisors have been active during the recent rise of SPACs, and there appears to be no regulatory or accreditation hurdle preventing their continued proliferation.

As previously indicated, the rise of "celebrity" SPACs prompted the SEC's Office of Investor Education and Advocacy to issue guidance in March 2021 explicitly warning investors to avoid investing in a SPAC based solely on celebrity endorsements or other information they receive through social media, online advertisements, investment newsletters, email, investment research websites, internet chat rooms, direct mail, magazines, newspapers, television or radio. Some SPAC sponsors currently include former baseball coach Billy Beane, popstar Ciara and basketball superstar Stephen Curry.

Investors should carefully evaluate the degree of involvement of a non-traditional SPAC participant and the degree to which their involvement is accompanied by proven industry or financial leadership. For example, Forest Road Acquisition II received attention for basketball superstar celebrity Shaquille O'Neal's contribution as a "strategic advisor," but SPAC is led by former Disney executives Kevin Mayer and Thomas Staggs, which probably fits well with SPAC's pursuit of a focus on technology, media, and telecommunications.

Quarterback Patrick Mahomes and pitcher Justin Verlander's role in Disruptive Acquisition Corp is limited to their membership on an "Athlete Advisory Council." Conversely, celebrities with a leadership role or who sit on SPAC's board may be a more significant cause for investor caution. Former baseball player Alex Rodriguez for example, as CEO of SPAC Slam Corp, may or may not prove to be an able SPAC manager; in either case, it is reasonable for investors to watch carefully given that his role extends well beyond an advisory capacity.

Rights' Decrease After The Merger

SPAC's buy-and-hold investors may have weaker rights when they become shareholders of the surviving company. The combined company after the SPAC merger may have weaker governance characteristics relative to SPAC. This decrease in rights is not entirely surprising, considering that the average SPAC shareholder stake in the merged firm is 35%, according to an estimated.

The impact may have long-term effects on the future of the combined company. For example, SPACs Kensington Capital and Diamond Eagle Acquisition were founded as single-share, single-vote entities before becoming dual-class companies with differentiated voting rights after completing SPAC mergers with QuantumScape DraftKings, respectively.

SPAC sponsors are not necessarily complicit in deteriorating governance practices. For example, SPAC sponsor David Hall resigned from the Velodyne Lidar board shortly after taking the company public through a SPAC merger. He publicly accused the Velodyne board of fostering what he described as an "anti-shareholder culture" that lacks public company experience, fails to prioritize shareholder value, and "rubber-stamps" executive compensation packages.

The SPAC model poses certain risks to investors, especially those who own SPAC shares through the de-SPAC merger.

Investors can mitigate their downside exposure by redeeming or selling their shares before the business combination or by negotiating a favorable underwriting agreement through a PIPE investment, which allows for a rigorous and confidential evaluation of the going concern. Over time, SPACs could become more appealing to investors who own shares through the business combination as disclosure and terms evolve to be more shareholder-friendly.

Bad Performances

There are some SPACs that go on to offer very strong returns. As indicated, one of the most successful so far is fantasy sports and betting company DraftKings (which merged with Diamond Eagle Acquisition SPAC back in April 2020). Its stock price is approaching $70, which is an amazing return for a $10 investment. And many others have provided returns of several hundred percent to investors.

But most SPACs are not doing so well. A 2020 academic study by the New York University School of Law reveals that most of them underperform the overall market after closing a deal. It's interesting to see how the results are generally much better for "high-quality sponsors," meaning individuals affiliated with a private asset fund with more than $1 billion in assets or who have been CEOs or other senior managers of a Fortune 500 company. On the same line, according to a Renaissance Capital study, 89 SPACs that had gone public since 2015 presented an average 18.5% loss. On the contrary, traditional IPOs booked an average gain of 37.2% over that same period of time.

SPACs vs. IPOs

We have talked about SPAC's general pros and cons; now we will focus on the main differences and the specific advantages and disadvantages of SPACs and traditional IPOs.

As you might already know, an IPO is a major move for a private company, and it permits it to access significant funds for its expansion without taking on debt. In exchange for this capital, the company will no longer be a privately owned one and will share its status to shareholder-owned.

As mentioned before, during the COVID-19 lockdown, IPO's global activity significantly slowed down, hitting an almost 50% volume decrease compared to the months of April and May 2019. But things quickly recovered, and 2020 saw the most significant IPO capital raising activity in ten years.

IPOs: How Do They Work?

First, a private company decides to sell shares to the public, and after an audit of its financials, paperwork is then filed with the SEC.

Next, the stock exchange reviews the company's application to conduct an IPO: this can be accepted, amended, or rejected.

In case everything is approved, the company has to decide the number of shares that will be sold on the chosen stock exchange. An investment bank then determines the IPO price after running an independent evaluation of the business. The initial share price is listed and released: the stock is finally available for public trading.

SPACs And IPOs Major Differences

On the other hand, SPACs work in the reverse order of an IPO. As indicated, they go public on the stock market by directly selling shares to the investors, and then they try to acquire a company with a 24-months deadline.

IPO's Pros

An IPO offers important visibility to a company, signaling its growth potential and success. And a successful IPO can be a good leverage to gain better terms when the company applies for loans.

Also, investors get in early, and for them, this is a chance to get in on the ground floor of a growing company. The investment may generate good returns, even in a short period of time.

The potential for long-term gains is also significant, exactly what happened in the case of Facebook. When the social media giant went public back in 2012, its stock opened at only $38/share. Currently, Facebook shares are trading at $257/share, marking an impressive 576% increase.

The IPO process is also transparent, and the share price is indicated in the documents so that all investors can see it in advance.

Furthermore, emerging companies generally discount their opening share price, which will be very affordable for investors. Just to make an example, back in 1997, when Amazon (AMZN) went public, its share price was only $18!

IPO's Cons

This is a long and expensive process. The company's executives lose quite some time filling in all the paperwork and requirements, and the company has to retain an investment bank. So this investment and the auditing and legal fees are all included in the costs of an IPO.

Also, after an IPO, company owners and entrepreneurs basically lose control of the business: the Board of Directors is now in the position to change the founding team. Not exactly a trivial detail.

Traditional IPOs are also riskier for investors if we compare them to blue-chip and established stocks with years of steady performances.

Last but not least, prices might plummet after an IPO; investors might find themselves with shares whose value is much inferior to the IPO price. This is exactly what happened to the ride-hailing service Lyft. LYFT shares crashed 22% on its second day of trading, and almost two years later, LYFT is still trading down 21% compared to its 72$ IPO price.

SPAC's Pros Compared To IPO

As we said, despite its downsides, SPACs' process is overall faster, less complicated, and less expensive for a company. Undoubtedly one of the major benefits of a SPAC compared to an IPO will always be that it allows companies to get the required capital in a shorter time and with better conditions. And also, as previously explained, that investors can redeem their shares for the 10$ price of the purchase plus interest if they don't agree with the proposed acquisition.

Furthermore, SPACS allow a company to provide future forecasts since projections are forward-looking. This cannot happen in a classic IPO prospectus due to the risk of liability. But since SPACs are basically a merger, they are in the position of indicating to the investors what the company will be like after the merger.

There are also more opportunities for investors, especially considering that the instability of the market has pushed SPACs to the front line. And those entrepreneurs that are worried the classic IPO route might damage their first attempt to go public can decide to merge with a SPAC instead.

Unlike what happens with IPOs, the target company and the SPAC first agree on a fixed valuation. And once the SPAC begins trading shares, this limits price volatility.

In any case, it is important to take into account that a SPAC might receive a lower valuation than an IPO and that it also has to pay the sponsor fee.

SPAC's Cons Compared To IPO

You should know by now that with SPACS, investors don't know the final acquisition target, and they have to trust the SPAC's managers and founders will pick the best target company.

SPACs can identify a certain business or industry in their IPO prospectus that they intend to target when seeking to combine with an operating company. Still, the truth is they are not obligated to pursue a merger in the indicated industry.

Another potential problem is that SPACs have 24 months to find and start the acquisition process. So even though investors will ultimately receive money and interests, they will have lost the potential returns of two years of active investments.

Returns are also generally weaker. Between 2015 and 2020, 93 out of 313 SPACs completed mergers and took a company public. According to Renaissance Capital, the common shared delivered a median -9.6% loss and an average 29.1% return. Traditional IPOs, instead, had a median return of 47.1% in that same period. Overall, just 29 SPACs of this group had positive returns.

SPACs can be risky to investors because companies don't always receive the due diligence and in-depth vetting of a classic IPO, and this can impact future performance.

Investors – especially retail ones – also face the risk of investing in startups that could not really be ready for public market activity.

In short, a traditional IPO is generally more likely than a SPAC to find out the true market value of a company at its time of listing. Classic IPOs also offer certain safeguards to investors whose enthusiasm for charismatic founders and brand new industries may outweigh the need to conduct due diligence or cloud their judgment about the right time for investing.

This doesn't mean at all that all SPACs are bad; actually, some of them have been doing just great. But some extra skepticism is recommended because it's likely that several bad targets will be coming to the market in the upcoming months while the really good ones become fewer and farther between. This is why doing your homework after a target is announced becomes more important than ever.

Which Companies Should Choose A SPAC Over An IPO And Why

This mostly has to do with the company's business nature.

Companies that have huge revenues, that are already very well established, are profitable, and extremely well known, they will most likely always pick up the IPO route.

But those companies that are in a slightly more early stage, a bit far from the proof of concept, belong to a sector which may be a bit complicated to understand... well they might really benefit from a SPAC since Special Purpose Acquisition Companies permit this kind of companies to share with the investors their upcoming business plan.

This is the case, for example, of electric-vehicle manufacturers and auto-tech companies: nowadays, there are plenty of them, and we all know that in 2040 there will probably be many more electric vehicles on the street than "traditional" ones. But what is still unclear is whose vehicles they will be. Well, in that light, this kind of company can use the SPAC route to explain their aim and goals better, allowing investors to understand what and how they are planning to do things over a certain period of time.

In any case, since the SPAC route can be faster, we could also see some companies with "IPO characteristics" choose the SPAC way.

SPAC Deal: What Kind Of Company Makes The Best Candidate?

Now, let's focus on the main characteristics of the ideal company for a SPAC merger.

As you probably already know, during 2020, the scope of SPAC targets has been expanding with deals getting done across different sectors: technology transactions, business services, industrial deals, consumer acquisitions, financial services transactions, healthcare, and energy deals.

But despite the variety of industries, all the ideal targets for successful mergers typically share the following points:

- Viable IPO candidates in their own right, typically in high-growth sectors, with interesting long-term prospects that long-term investors would see as an attractive opportunity, and the proper management and infrastructure team to support the obligations of being a public company.

- Companies that seek a path to liquidity and access to capital even in difficult debt and equity markets, the likelihood and duration of which are uncertain.

- Companies seeking quick access to the public markets with limited market or timing risk, flexibility to manage complicated structures, and access to a team of sponsors.

- Targets that have succession issues or could be over-leveraged or simply want to maintain majority ownership and upside potential and can be structured through an earn-out.

SPACs Investing: The Different Stages Of The Deal

In order to understand how SPAC negotiations work, we need to recap and focus a bit more on all the players involved and what their leverage and motivations are.

SPAC's sponsors (founders) purchase 20% of SPAC's shares in exchange for a nominal consideration as compensation for the start-up of SPAC. The founders control the SPAC Board of Directors.

SPAC's public shareholders who bought in the initial public offering or in the trading market own 80% of the shares they acquired at $10 per share and warrants to buy more shares at $11.50 per share. (It is almost always $10 per share and $11.50 exercise price for the warrants.) Shareholders generally must give the merger the green light, and they are also entitled to have their shares redeemed for $10/share if they don't like the fusion agreement. Therefore, most of the time, the deal has to please them.

What makes this more complicated is the fact that the funds the SPAC holds in trust to redeem shares from the public at $10 per share are often less than the amount needed to redeem all of them. Underwriting and other SPAC operating fees and expenses may have reduced the trust fund by 20% to 30%. Therefore, SPACs need to avoid massive redemptions or raise more money to fund redemptions.

In addition, many SPAC transactions involve PIPES (Private Investments in Public Equity) investors. The PIPES investors add additional money to the SPAC that comes in when the merger closes. The SPAC negotiates with the PIPES investors, while the SPAC negotiates the terms of the merger with the private target company. Therefore, the merger negotiation is often a three-way thing because the PIPES investors have leverage that affects the terms of the merger.

Now, let's talk about the target company. Different groups affect their negotiating position. Members of the management team may have one objective.

Investors holding different classes of stock with different rights to cash and stock received in the merger may have other objectives. SPACs require major investors and the management team to commit to voting to give the merger the green light at the time the merger agreement is signed and not to sell to third parties. This is because the SPAC does not want to announce a deal publicly and then not be able to close it because the target company's shareholders will not approve it.

So, a successful SPAC merger has to satisfy all of the following groups: SPAC sponsors, PIPES investors, public shareholders, public warrant holders, the target company's management team, and the various classes of target company investors.

The PIPES investors are the ultimate money in the deal. For them, it is important to be the first to cash in. Therefore, PIPES investors obtain registration rights and demand lock-up agreements from the other participants to ensure that they have the first opportunity to sell shares in the public market.

It is all quite complex and expensive with so many interests at play, but undoubtedly for the right companies, it can work. The best thing about SPACs is that the negotiation occurs before the SPAC publicly announces the transaction.

The price and other terms are set when the merger agreement is signed. If negotiations break down and a merger agreement is not reached, it is not a public event like filing with the U.S. Securities and Exchange Commission for an IPO and then not being able to seal the deal.

Obviously, since SPACs are public companies, they are affected by the change of market conditions. Therefore, there is no absolute guarantee that one of the groups will not later try to renegotiate the agreement.

So who pays if everything falls apart? The target company pays its own fees, and the SPAC pays its own. This means that if the deal falls to pieces, the target company may have wasted plenty of money.

Talking about money, let's now try to understand the time and money needed to close a SPAC deal. So, first of all, you should be aware that almost all the SPAC merger time schedules that can be found online are somehow misleading.

Why? Basically, because of two things. First, they do not include the three to six months it usually takes for the SPAC and the private company to get to know each other to decide if the deal makes sense and prepare the target company to successfully carry out the deal and be a public company. Next, most timetables assume that nothing will go wrong or make things go slower after the merger deal work gets more intense.

And so this means that it might be necessary to add three to six months to the schedules shown on the Internet to obtain a realistic picture of when it is necessary to start planning a SPAC transaction.

Getting ready for the SPAC or IPO transaction requires management money and time. Therefore, it is crucial to know how long it is likely to take to receive the money and how much cash is going to be spent on transaction expenses and preparing everything to operate a public company.

How much does a SPAC merger transaction cost for the target company?

We are generally talking about at least $200,000 in legal and accounting fees during the last few months of the merger transaction.

What is spent before, during the preparation period, generally depends on the target company's prior preparation. Do the accountants have the necessary qualifications to audit the financial statements to be filed with the SEC? Are SEC-compliant audited financial statements available? How much will it take to upgrade information technology systems to bring them up to public company standards?

The last months of the process can then be broken into different stages.

The first step is generally a letter of intent or a non-binding term sheet that details the structure and general terms of the agreement. Let's start from this date.

Over the next four to six weeks, while the potential transaction remains a secret, SPAC completes the due diligence it initiated during the preparation period, the merger agreement is negotiated, and the target company's shareholders sign the voting agreements.

There may also be presentations to sell the deal to PIPES investors to raise more money than is in the SPAC trust fund. Selling the deal to PIPES investors is usually the main reason for the delay, and at this point, the accord is still confidential.

After the merger agreement is signed, the process of "de-SPACing" begins, i.e., the process of transforming a SPAC into a real company.

At this point (4-6 weeks after the letter of intent), during a press release, the SPAC announces the agreement and files a Form 8-K with the U.S. Securities and Exchange Commission, and then it files a proxy statement and registration statement with the same SEC.

While waiting for the SEC reviewers to sign off on the settlement (and hope that plaintiffs' lawyers do not initiate litigation seeking a better deal for public SPAC shareholders), it is necessary to work on a new listing application to get the SPAC-devoid shares listed on the NASDAQ or NYSE.

Then we should calculate another 7 weeks, so that by the time official shareholder meeting notices are sent out, we will be 15 weeks into the process.

About four weeks later, SPAC's public shareholders approve the merger, and about 17 weeks into the process, the closing takes place.

The brand new company then files a Super 8-K with the U.S. Securities and Exchange Commission, and the shares of the divested SPAC Company start trading on a new list.

The next step is the registration statement for the resale of PIPE investor shares. This registration statement usually takes several weeks to become effective because the SEC staff has recently reviewed the merger-related documents.

For approx.180 days following the completion of the SPAC process, the sponsor's and target company's shareholders are locked out and cannot trade. In some SPAC transactions, the lock-ups are longer or could be subject to market price milestones that shorten or lengthen this time.

And since the SPAC was a public shell company, investors cannot use Rule 144 to resell shares until after one year after the Super 8-K filing.

What can companies do to keep the deal on schedule or even get deals done more quickly?

The best thing would be to do as much as possible in the preparation period. Like, for example, choosing the right SPAC to sell the deal to public shareholders and PIPES investors. Also, keeping an eye on the management of the company while the deal is going through.

But always keeping in mind that adverse and unexpected changes before the closing may delay the entire operation.

SPACs Investing: The Most Important Tips For Beginners

As indicated, more and more SPACS are coming to market these days, and that leaves plenty of choices to pick from when analyzing the potential reward site. And as we know that no target has been announced yet, we will talk about the main things to take into account when considering a SPAC investment, mainly focusing on three major points: the investors behind it, its size, and the target industry.

But first of all, you should ask yourself: are you willing to commit trading capital to a stock when you don't know yet what you are actually buying? Some investors actually find this mystery exciting; others may have some more doubts. In any case, don't forget that if things don't go the way you would have wanted to, you can always ask your money back when a SPAC finally merges.

Also, even though SPACs can't indicate to their investors the specific business they are planning to buy when the SPAC does its IPO, they do describe factors like geography and industry and development stage. And even though, as we have just seen, there might be exceptions, they normally stick to it. Every SPAC seeking a merger has a little profile that is available to read for free. And you can find out much more about each SPAC by looking at SPAC filings with the SEC or hiring an adviser or an investment banker.
According to The SEC's Office of Investor Education and Advocacy (OIEA), whether you invest in a SPAC by choosing to participate in its IPO or by acquiring its securities on the open market following an IPO, you should read very well the SPAC's IPO prospectus, and also its reports, both current and periodic, filed with the U.S. Securities and Exchange Commission pursuant to its ongoing reporting obligations.

It is crucial to fully understand the terms of your investment. Although SPACs are often structured in a very similar way and may be subject to certain minimum listing requirements, it is vital to be aware of the specifics of each particular one, like the equity interests held by the sponsor, which may have been obtained for a nominal consideration.

Also, since, for its own nature, SPACs do not present operating histories to evaluate, it is fundamental to review the business background of the sponsors and SPAC's management. And it is possible to find SPACS' IPO prospectus, as well as current and periodic reports on the SEC's EDGAR database.

Also, SPACs typically invest the proceeds in overall safe interest-bearing instruments, but it is important to be careful and always review the specific terms of an offering, as there is no rule indicating that the proceeds must be invested only in those kinds of instruments.

SPACs typically use the interest on trust account investments to pay taxes.

As indicated, in connection with a business combination, a SPAC offers its investors the opportunity to redeem their shares instead of becoming shareholders of the combined company. And if the SPAC fails to complete the business combination, the shareholders are beneficiaries of the trust and are entitled to their pro-rata share of the total amount then on deposit in the trust account. But one important thing to keep in mind is that if you have acquired your SPAC shares on the open market, then you are just granted your proportionate share of the trust account and not at the price you purchased the SPAC shares. Let's make an example: if a SPAC had an IPO at $10/share, but you purchased 100 shares of SPAC stock on the open market at $12/share, those shares you bought are linked to a trust

account balance of about $10/share. This means that your share of the trust account would be worth about $1,000 and not the $1,200 you actually paid for your shares.
This is why you should always go over the SPAC IPO prospectus to properly understand the terms of the trust account, like the circumstances under which cash may be released from the account and your redemption rights.

What else? Well, as we said before, every SPAC has a sponsor or group of sponsors (also known as founders) who organized the SPAC. They attract investors based on their track record and reputation. So, always look at their past records - were their previous operations successful? Or did they go under? Once again, please stay away from celebrity sponsors, those sports and entertainment figures who lend their names to attract investors to SPACs. Instead, lean toward SPACs sponsored by people who have built successful public companies in the industry of interest.
In short, look for a high-quality management team since this is basically who you are giving your money to. At the same time, even though having diligent investors on board is crucial, a well-known name, someone that is like a brand themselves in that particular field, is also a guarantee to get the hype going and investors excited.
This is because playing SPACs prior to an announced target is about speculation and market mechanics; it is not yet about investing, and this is why it us fundamental to leverage hype whenever possible.
Then, as mentioned, you will have to be sure the SPAC targets an industry you are interested in. While you cannot know what the ultimate target is going to be, the concept of the target industry will at least offer you some idea of the kind of company you might end up investing in, be it electric vehicles, space tourism, fintech, or something completely different.

It is also extremely important to have an idea of the SPAC's size. While big amounts of money are likely to draw attention because larger SPACs will have to target bigger companies, this can also be a limitation in the universe of choices. Just to make an example, a 1.5-billion $ SPAC will probably not target a company worth 250 million $ and vice versa. While a PIPE (private investment in public equity) round can sum up to the size of the SPAC in case of need, you won't really know to what extent that could happen if you are trying to get in as close to the ground level as possible.

Another important suggestion would be: spread the bet. Since, at this stage, it's unknown what you are getting, it is advisable to avoid targeting just one single SPAC. Instead, it is important to determine how much money you want to allocate to SPACs and that divide that amount among different ones and of different sizes. This way, it will be easier to increase the world of potential targets. Where to find possible candidates? A pretty easy way is to use a website called "SPAC Track," where you can find all the information about the different SPACs, including key dates.

Valuation and dilution should also be kept in mind. As indicated, the search fees and underwriting may end up reducing the money in the trust, so it is crucial to keep up to date on the filings.
Once the target is announced, it is no longer possible to rely on the hype game. At that moment, you will have to get down to business and do some real diligence on the company, exactly like you would have done for any other investment. You will also have to remember that no matter the valuation you are told the deal was done at is based on the units' price of the IPO

(as we said before, generally $10), so if shares are above this amount, we will have to adjust the numbers.

Furthermore, when the business combination is finalized, founders' shares will come into play and weaken your ownership. So that $10 cash floor that represents your safety net will begin to go lower. Actually, according to a recent study, even though SPACs value their shares at $10 when the merge takes place, at the actual moment of the merger, the average SPAC has cash at its disposal for just $6.67/share.

As previously mentioned, we shouldn't forget about the inherent conflict of interest of the SPAC structure itself. Actually, this is probably the single most crucial thing to understand about SPACs' investing. Since insiders only see those founders' shares come into play once the business combination is over and considering that they pay almost nothing for those shares (don't forget that $25,000 is the aggregate cost of the founders' shares entitling them to ~20% of the outstanding shares after the merger), the one thing SPAC sponsors don't want to do is return the money, as they would be much better off financially by filing a "suboptimal" deal, than admitting defeat, giving the money back to the investors, and never seeing the founders' shares come into play. After all, they paid almost nothing for that ~20% ownership.

Above all, the most important filters to take into account when considering investing in a SPAC would be the following ones:

- A well-known management team that possibly counts with a highly recognizable name
- An interesting target industry with good potential
- Pre-split units
- As close to 10$/share as possible

- Diversification
- Eyes open for conflict of interests and dilutions

In general, especially if you are a beginner, keep in mind: a SPAC is just an instrument for a private company to go public. But the important thing here is the fundamentals of this company. If a strong and growing one chooses a SPAC to go public, then it has a real chance of long-term success. If an overnight operation with high hopes but no revenues uses a SPAC, the results will most likely be very poor. So do your researches!

Where Investors Can Buy SPACs

As we said, SPAC sponsors have up to 24 months to acquire a company, and this can make it difficult for an investor to find active SPACs.

This is why you will have to rely on a resource such as the regularly updated list of active and pre-IPO SPACs. SPAC Track, for example, provides a comprehensive list of all active or pre-IPO SPACs, with the names of their sponsors, target sector, and other useful information.

Once you've identified a few interesting SPACs, you can head over to the brokers' website Robinhood and look for the SPAC you want to buy. But watch out. You have to search for the specific form you want to acquire. What does it mean? That if you start searching by ticker alone, you'll only buy shares of the trust, not whole units. So if you want to buy whole units, look for the ticker symbol and add a "U." For warrants, add the letter "W" instead. Then you can place an order to buy SPAC units in the same way you would place any other order on this website.

Remember that while you can buy and hold SPACs until the merger occurs, this strategy over the long term might be pretty risky: a study found that up to 50% of SPAC acquisitions end in losses for investors.

Despite this, many investors are still attracted to the high upside potential if they end up with a good buy. But you should know that you can still profit from SPACs without taking on as much risk by using a short-term strategy. And there are two possible ways to do this.

The first option you have is to sell the whole unit, just as you would sell any other stock. So you buy it at its current market price, you wait for the price to rise, and then you sell it at a higher one. This implies practically the same risks as any other short-term trade.

Your second option is to split the unit into its components (share and warrant). And when the unit is split, you can sell them separately on the open market. This can be a profitable strategy if the current market price of shares and warrants is higher than the price at which you bought the warrant. However, remember that every SPAC has its own guidelines as to when a unit can be split. When the split date arrives, you can ask your broker to split the units. And if they charge a commission for that, factor it into any possible profit, you expect to make by splitting your units.

The websites Webull and SoFi are also good alternatives for investors.

SPAC Trends In 2021

First of all, we should say that among the SPACs with a specific industry focus, the trend is toward aiming at technology companies, which represent more than 25% since January 1st, 2020.

Other industries of interest such as health care, life science, energy, consumer services, and financial services are also often aiming at the technology-related sectors of those industries. We are talking about biotech, pharma/medtech, electric vehicles and cleantech, fintech, and industrial and government tech.

This trend towards technology and early-stage companies makes totally sense, as these are often in need of substantial capital. The companies that are in a better position to take advantage of the unique combinations of features, which SPACs can offer, are those needing both a large influx of capital and access to liquidity.

And talking about numbers in 2021, by May of this same year, there were more than 300 listed SPACs generating gross proceeds of more than $100 billion. The most impressive thing is that this amount has already surpassed the total proceeds from SPACs in the previous year.

An example of this is 23andMe, a consumer genetic-testing company whose CEO, Anne Wojcicki, announced in February 2021 the intent to go public through V.G. Acquisition, a SPAC founded by Richard Branson. Each of them would contribute $25 million to the SPAC and expect to raise $759 million from private and public investors to fund the acquisition of 23andMe. According to Wojcicki, she chose the SPAC route because this gave her the possibility to know in advance who her investors are, unlike what would have happened with an IPO where going public comes first.

Overall, we could say that despite the recent "SPAC crash," SPACs are enjoying another record year, and several private equities (PE) and venture capital (VC) firms have shown increasing interest in incorporating SPACs into their investment and structuring toolkits.

In many respects, the aims of SPACs and customary VC / PE strategies are quite similar, and firms are now realizing that SPACs can offer several advantages compared to the classic acquisition and investment holding structures utilized by PE.

2021 has already witnessed a number of PE backed SPAC launches, as well as announcements of proposed PE SPACs, which in total could amount to many billions of dollars in IPO proceeds. If these SPACs should be successful, then they could become a major part of how PE does business over the next ten years or more.

SPARCs (Special Purpose Acquisition Rights Companies): What Are They?

Talking about the present (and the future) of SPACS, we can't forget about the newest "trends" of all: *SPARCS*.

What exactly are they?

Back in July 2020, billionaire Bill Ackman created the $4 billion special purpose acquisition vehicle (SPAC) Pershing Square Tontine Holdings Ltd.

But after nearly a year without a deal, in the spring of 2021, the SPAC announced that it would acquire a 10% stake in Universal Music Group, which is majority-owned by French conglomerate Vivendi S.E. for about $4 billion. The Universal acquisition deal will not be a typical SPAC deal, in which a SPAC merges with a private company causing this one to become a listed company in its own right. Universal will be listed on Euronext Amsterdam, and PSTH will get a 10% stake in the public company.

The SPAC had approximately $1.6 billion of additional funds available from the exercise of its Forward Purchase Agreements with the Pershing Square Funds and its affiliates.

Upon completion of the transaction, the SPAC, named PSTH Remainco, will be left with $1.5 billion. Ackman's company will also create a new entity called Pershing Square SPARC Holdings, Ltd.

So, SPARC stands for a special purpose acquisition *rights* company. Unlike traditional SPACs, which first raise capital from investors and then seek to invest in a private company to take it public within 24 months, a SPARC will first identify the target company, and then investors can determine whether they want to invest in it or not.

SPARCs will have the advantage of reduced time pressure, as they will not be subject to the 24-month deadline to close a transaction and minimal underwriting costs.

SPARCs also intend to issue rights to acquire shares of SPARC common stock for $20.00 per share to PSTH shareholders. Ackman's SPARC will have a minimum of $6.6 billion in cash and about $10.6 billion to fund any future transaction.

Conclusions

In conclusion, SPACs are poised to continue growing in 2021. Investors and private companies are more comfortable with the model, and the increasing demand will probably encourage more financial and business executives to continue sponsoring their own SPACs.

In addition, the 2020 frenzy has created many SPACs that have not yet merged with other companies. This means that SPAC supply is high, and private companies and their sponsors have a pool of opportunities to debut in the public market.

At the same time, in the United States, SPACs may face increased regulatory scrutiny under the Joe Biden administration, particularly from Treasury Secretary Janet Yellen, who has expressed concern about rollbacks in financial regulation under the Trump administration.

It is true that SPACS have slowed down if compared to the prior quarters, but this figure alone is not a conclusive indicator of the viability of the asset class itself.

According to Morningstar analyst Ruth Saldanha, the pace of new special purpose acquisition company deals may appear to have slowed in the second quarter of 2021, but she believes that SPACs are here to stay. According to PitchBook data, 13 SPACs have closed between April 1 and April 15, 2021, in addition to the other 316 in the first quarter of 2021. And we should expect many more.

Overall, the most exciting thing to see from now on is how SPACs will evolve. Will the balance of risk/reward for investors vs. management get better? And will SPARCs take over from SPACs? In any case, most indicators point to a pretty healthy market in 2021, with growing demand for SPACs. And with all the innovative SPAC deals taking place lately, this trend shouldn't be going away any time soon...

CITED SOURCES

Klausner, Ohlrogge & Ruan: A Sober Look at SPACs. NYU Law and Economics Research Paper (March 2021).

Vinson & Elkins, LLP., Harvard Law School Forum on Corporate Governance: Update on Special Purpose Acquisition Companies (August 17, 2020).

U.S. Securities and Exchange Commission, Investors Alerts and Bulletins: Celebrity Involvement with SPACs – Investor Alert (March 10, 2021).

U.S. Securities and Exchange Commission, Investors Alerts and Bulletins: **What You Need to Know About SPACs – Updated Investor Bulletin (May 25, 2021).**

U.S. Securities and Exchange Commission, Public Statements: John Coates, SPACs, IPOs and Liability Risk under the Securities Laws – (April 8, 2021).

Renaissance Capital, SPAC returns fall short of traditional IPO returns on average (July 28, 2020).

Ruth Saldanha: SPACs Are Here to Stay. MorningStar (May 7, 2021) .

www.ingramcontent.com/pod-product-compliance
Lightning Source LLC
Chambersburg PA
CBHW070454220526
45466CB00004B/1828